ANIMAL EMOTIONS

WHEN MONKEYS LAUGH

HEATHER MOORE NIVER

Enslow Publishing
101 W. 23rd Street
Suite 240
New York, NY 10011
USA
enslow.com

WORDS TO KNOW

aggression Angry or forceful actions toward another.

anthropologist A scientist who studies human beings.

anthropomorphize To give human features to animals.

bond Something that brings two or more things together.

contagious Spread from one thing or person to another.

dominant The most important or powerful.

expression The appearance of the face that shows emotion.

hyena A mammal from Africa that looks a lot like a dog.

mammal A warm-blooded animal.

primate A mammal that has hands and feet that can grip, a large brain, and vision.

submission Giving in.

CONTENTS

CHAPTER ONE

TICKLED TOES

An amazing sight occurred in the Sacred Monkey Forest located on the Indonesian island of Bali. In 2011, a long-tailed macaque seemed to be tickling its own feet and laughing! At first the scientists thought the monkey was enjoying a satisfying scratch of its itchy toes. But then the macaque's face broke into a wide grin! Scientists began to wonder if the monkey

Going Ape!

Monkeys look a lot like apes, but they have some differences. All monkeys have tails, for example. Sometimes their tails are just a tiny stump. Apes do not have tails. Chimpanzees, orangutans, and gorillas are all apes.

This bonobo is a type of chimpanzee. As you can see, bonobos also seem to laugh.

was laughing! If you've ever tried to tickle your own toes, you know it's not easy. So scientists have continued to study monkeys and apes.

Many **primates** seem to laugh and smile. Chimpanzees, bonobos, gorillas, and orangutans have all been recorded making sounds like laughter

When orangutans laugh it sounds more like panting than human laughter.

when they are tickled. Their responses to tickling sounded a lot like human laughing. Chimps and bonobos are closely related to humans. So it may not be a big surprise that their laughter sounds the most like human laughter. Gorillas and orangutans are not such close relatives to humans. And their laughs are very different.

Fact

Scientists are studying all mammals to see if they all have a sense of humor, too.

The animal kingdom has many kinds of monkeys: baboons, drills, mandrills, macaques, guenons, langurs, colobus monkeys, marmosets, tamarins, howler monkeys, spider monkeys, squirrel monkeys, woolly monkeys, and capuchins.

CHAPTER TWO

HUMOROUS HISTORY

Studies of animal emotions go back for many years. Many scientists study whether or not animals have feelings like we do. One of the most famous scientists to study animal emotions was Charles Darwin. Darwin felt that animals and humans were both pretty smart. He also thought that animals and humans probably had a sense of humor, too. Darwin studied grinning dogs and monkeys that laughed when they were tickled.

More Emotions

Some scientists think all mammals might have a sense of humor. Even insects such as honeybees might have emotions. Studies show that these sweet-making bees feel different levels of happiness and sadness.

Jane Goodall studied chimpanzees closely. She noticed that chimps make a breathing sound like laughter when they play.

Fact

Spiders have different personalities, ranging from timid to aggressive.

More recently, Jane Goodall famously studied and lived with chimpanzees. She saw that the young chimps let off a kind of breathy sound when they played. It seems a lot like human laughter. **Anthropologist** Barbara J. King has also studied animal emotions and believes that many animals and birds probably feel emotions like we do.

We have to be careful when we study animals, say some scientists. It is very easy to assume animals act just like we do. Thinking of animals as having the same qualities as humans is called **anthropomorphizing**. It's important to remember that monkeys and other animals might not laugh in the same way or for the same reasons we do. But scientists think that monkeys and other animals probably have similar positive emotions. And negative ones, too!

CHAPTER THREE

FUNNY FACE

Primates have faces that are very similar to human faces. This makes it a little easier to tell when monkeys and apes are showing emotions like smiling and laughing.

Apes smile and laugh a lot like we do. They have two basic **expressions** to show when they are smiling or laughing. Sometimes they bare, or show, their teeth. It's similar to a human smile. They use

Koko the Jokester

A gorilla named Koko knows how to joke with words. When she is asked to describe things that are hard, she signs "rock" and "work." She also once tied her trainer's shoelaces together. Then she signed "chase!"

this expression when they tickle each other or want to make another ape feel good. Apes also seem to laugh with an open mouth. They do this when they play.

Fact

Scientists think that a sense of humor shows that chimpanzees have feelings and intelligence similar to ours.

Chimpanzees may show their teeth and smile when they laugh, like humans do. They may or may

This Barbary ape's face shows an expression that humans associate with a smile.

not make any sound when they laugh. Chimps also smile and laugh when they play. These grins and giggles probably show that they are having a good time!

Chimpanzees seem to show their teeth when they smile or laugh. This seems a lot like human behavior.

Koko the gorilla has learned more than two thousand words and one thousand American Sign Language signs. She makes laughing sounds when she sees a human acting clumsy. She has a special laughing sound for her favorite visitors, too. It sounds like "ho ho."

CHAPTER FOUR

SLEEPY SMILES

Humans laugh all the time, but what is laughter? According to scientists, it's the body's reaction as a result of an event. This response is one you can hear and see. Muscles in your stomach and respiratory system work hard when you laugh. There are two kinds of laughter. Social laughter is caused by things you find funny, like a joke. Another kind of laughter

Be Careful When You Smile at a Monkey

In the monkey world, showing your teeth is sometimes a sign of anger. Other signs of aggression in monkeys include head bobbing, yawning, and shaking their heads and shoulders forward.

This sleepy eastern chimpanzee is spontaneously smiling. Spontaneous smiles happen when the animal is unaware of its actions, like when sleeping.

When some monkeys, like this langur, show their teeth, they are not joyful! They want to scare off threatening animals.

is a result of a physical trigger, like being tickled.

Sometimes people seem to laugh and smile in their sleep. Their faces move to show smiling. These sleepy smiles are called spontaneous smiles. With animals, this happens when they are not aware of what they are doing, like sleeping. Chimpanzees and baby Japanese macaques have also been seen showing spontaneous smiles.

Scientists think these movements during sleep are related to how humans began to smile and laugh in the first place. Humans and primates have a lot in common. Some scientists who have studied primates believe that our relatives who lived thirty million years ago (or more!) might have smiled and laughed, too. They might not have used the "ha ha ha" kind of laughter we know today, though.

Fact

Other animals might smile in their sleep, too. Scientists have yet to catch them in the act!

CHAPTER FIVE

CONTAGIOUS CACKLING

Monkeys often smile at each other during regular everyday activities, a lot like humans do.

Monkeys and humans also smile out of fear. When you see a dog showing its teeth, it's best to back off. This is a sign of **aggression**. But in the monkey world, teeth may mean something else sometimes. In a study of rhesus macaques, scientists saw a lot of bared teeth. But it wasn't a sign that a

Getting the Giggles

Studies have shown that rats make laughing noises as they play together. These sounds occur when they are chasing one another and wrestling. They also seem to laugh when they are tickled.

fight was about to start. When there was tension between two monkeys, the less **dominant** one often smiled. Then the more dominant aggressive monkey became more pleasant. So when one monkey was afraid, it did what is called "fear grinning."

Have you ever found it impossible to keep from laughing? This may happen in the primate world, too.

The baboon showing its teeth might be "fear grinning" to make its more aggressive partner calm down.

This brown woolly monkey might smile to show others that it is in a good mood.

Sometimes laughter is **contagious**, kind of like when you see someone else yawn and you have to yawn! You can't help it.

When young apes are playing, they have what looks like a happy face. When other apes see it, they often join in the fun with a similar expression. They make happy-sounding noises, too. These noises are also a way primates communicate with one another. The laughing shows other primates their mood.

Fact

Rats do not laugh the same way when tickled by something much larger. It is more like being bullied.

CHAPTER SIX

A CHIMP CONNECTION

Studies of chimpanzees show that they laugh when they are playing and having fun together.

Chimpanzees laugh to **bond**. They also laugh with other chimps as a response, similar to what humans do when they are having a conversation. It's a laugh that shows they are listening. But chimps don't laugh just because they hear others chuckling. They only laugh if they are a part of the group having fun.

No Faking Funny

Have you ever laughed at a joke you didn't understand or didn't think was all that funny? Fake laughter is not part of monkey life. So when monkeys and other primates laugh, they really find something funny!

Monkeys laugh for a short period of time in response to other monkeys. This is called responsive laughter. Think about when you are having a conversation with a friend.

Fact

After smiling at a dominant monkey, a submissive monkey will often move its body to show it is cooperative.

When chimpanzees play together, their laughter might be a way they bond, or connect with one another.

Macaque monkeys sometimes smile to show others that they are not threatening.

Sometimes you just laugh a little to show you are paying attention or understand.

When chimpanzees (or human beings) find something funny, they laugh longer. This is called compulsive laughter.

Have you ever laughed when you were nervous or scared? Macaque monkeys might do this, too. Their laughter might be a way to communicate **submission**. For example, when they feel threatened by another monkey, they laugh or smile. This grin shows the other monkey that they are afraid. The smiles might help avoid a fight between the two monkeys.

CHAPTER SEVEN

NO FAIR!

Monkeys feel more than joy and happiness, of course. Like humans, they also notice when things are unfair. In one study, monkeys showed that they might be able to tell whether or not they are treated fairly. Scientists asked monkeys to hand them a rock. They got a treat in return. The monkeys were happy to get a slice of cucumber at first. But they became annoyed if they saw another monkey getting a yummier snack, like a grape.

Mischievous Monkey

A crested black macaque got her hands on a photographer's camera! She took more than one hundred photographs of herself. At first, she bared her teeth. She had never seen her reflection before.

Crested macaque monkeys may be able to "read" one another's facial expressions. They know how other monkeys feel just based on their faces.

Fact

Dogs also seem to notice if another dog is getting different treatment. They begin to act differently if they are not rewarded and another dog is.

They would throw out the rock and the food. Finally the frustrated monkey would stop cooperating with the scientists at all.

Studies of crested macaque monkeys in Indonesia show that they can "read" the facial expressions of other monkeys. They can tell when one feels stress, anxiety, or anger. They yawn to show when they are anxious or stressed. Sometimes their faces look like they are screaming. Macaques use this expression when another monkey is being aggressive toward them. When they mean to threaten another macaque, they look at them with a half-open mouth.

CHAPTER EIGHT

PET SOUNDS

Of all the animals known to laugh, the laughter of chimps, gorillas, and apes sounds the most like a human laugh. Apes might make sounds like pants, grunts, or purrs. Even though other animals seem to laugh, it may sound very different than what we are used to hearing.

No Laughing Matter

You may have heard of a laughing hyena. But the sounds they make aren't because of a good joke. Hyenas make their laugh-like sound to communicate. They share information such as their age or how important they are in their group.

If this snowy owl were tickled, it would laugh. It would sound very different than human laughter, though.

Fact

Camels, dogs, owls, and penguins all seem to laugh when tickled. Scientists think some animals react to the feeling on their skin, like an itch. This is called knismesis.

It seems like dogs pant because they need extra breath. Maybe panting in short bursts is for that purpose. But dogs sometimes use long, loud pants. Scientists think these might be Fido's laughter. When dogs hear the sounds of other dogs making these longer, louder sounds, they seem to enjoy it. They become calm and listen closely.

Rat laughter is much too high for our ears to notice. When rats are tickled, they make a high-pitched sound. Scientists use special tools to detect these sounds. Some rats followed the human hand

Is this camel laughing? Scientists are not sure. Camels may be reacting to an itch or scratching on its skin.

that tickled them. They enjoyed being tickled and wanted more playtime!

Dolphins are some of the planet's smartest animals. It is almost impossible to tell by looking at them if they are laughing. But we know they have a sense of humor. Dolphins play jokes on some of their fellow fish. They have also played tricks on humans!

LEARN MORE

Books

Buchanan, Shelley. *Animal Senses.* Huntington Beach, CA: Teacher Created Materials, 2016.

Kopp, Megan. *The Language of Chimpanzees and Other Primates.* New York, NY: Cavendish Square, 2017.

Niver, Heather Moore. *Chimps and Monkeys Are NOT Pets.* New York, NY: Gareth Stevens, 2014.

Owen, Ruth. *Mischievous Monkeys.* New York, NY: Windmill Books, 2013.

Websites

Animal Fact Guide

animalfactguide.com/links

Check out photos, videos, and facts about animals from all over the globe.

How Animals Sound When They Laugh

mentalfloss.com/uk/animals/30752/how-animals-sound-when-they-laugh

Watch videos of different animals and see how their laughs compare to ours!

National Geographic: Gorilla Talk

video.nationalgeographic.com/video/exploreorg/gorilla-talk-eorg

See how gorillas talk using words and their bodies.

INDEX

Published in 2018 by Enslow Publishing, LLC.
101 W. 23rd Street, Suite 240, New York, NY 10011

Library of Congress Cataloging-in-Publication Data

Names: Niver, Heather Moore, author.
Title: When monkeys laugh / Heather Moore Niver.
Description: New York : Enslow Publishing, 2018. | Series: Animal emotions | Includes bibliographical references and index. | Audience: Grades 3 to 5.
Identifiers: LCCN 2017003415| ISBN 9780766086197 (library-bound) | ISBN 9780766088610 (pbk.) | ISBN 9780766088559 (6-pack)
Subjects: LCSH: Monkeys—Psychology—Juvenile literature. | Monkeys—Behavior—Juvenile literature. | Emotions in animals—Juvenile literature. | Laughter—Juvenile literature.
Classification: LCC QL737.P9 N58 2017 | DDC 599.8–dc23
LC record available at https://lccn.loc.gov/2017003415

Printed in the United States of America

To Our Readers: We have done our best to make sure all website addresses in this book were active and appropriate when we went to press. However, the author and the publisher have no control over and assume no liability for the material available on those websites or on any websites they may link to. Any comments or suggestions can be sent by e-mail to customerservice@enslow.com.

Photo Credits: Cover, p. 1 Fuse/Corbis/Getty Images; p. 5 Mint Images/Frans Lanting/Getty Images; p. 6 DLILLC/CorbisDocumentary/VCG/Getty Images; p. 9 Attila Kisbenedek/AFP/Getty Images; p. 12 JOHNGOMEZPIX/iStock/Thinkstock; p. 13 Steve Bloom Images/Alamy Stock Photo; p. 15 Cyril Ruoso/Minden Pictures/Getty Images; pp. 16, 4, 8, 11, 14, 18, 21, 24, 27 Ger Bosma/Moment Open/Getty Images; p. 19 Thomas Marent/Minden Pictures/Getty Images; p. 20 Tony Camacho/Science Source; p. 22 Anup Shah/The Image Bank/Getty Images; p. 23 Gabi Siebenhuehner/Shutterstock.com; p. 25 Barcroft Media/Getty Images; p. 28 Jim_Pintar/iStock/Thinkstock; p. 30 davidevison/iStock/Thinkstock; interior pages background image De Space Studio/Shutterstock.com.